Dull Men of Great Britain

Celebrating the Ordinary

LELAND CARLSON

EBURY
PRESS

3 5 7 9 10 8 6 4 2

This edition published 2015
First published in 2015 by Ebury Press, an imprint of Ebury Publishing
A Random House Group company

Ebury Press is part of the Penguin Random House group of companies whose addresses can be
found at global.penguinrandomhouse.com

The Random House Group Limited Reg. No. 954009

Addresses for companies within the Random House Group can be found at www.randomhouse.co.uk

A CIP catalogue record for this book is available from the British Library

ISBN 9781785030901

Printed and bound in Italy by Printer Trento S.r.l.

To buy books by your favourite authors and register for offers visit www.randomhouse.co.uk

CONTENTS

FOREWORD

The men featured in this book might strike you as passionate about things you regard as rather unusual, perhaps even dull or boring. For a variety of reasons, however, they may have stumbled upon an answer to the question of what makes for a happy life, and at the same time found an antidote to some of the ills of the 21st century.

An unlikely alliance of psychology, philosophy, neuroscience and Buddhism suggests that happiness lies not in the acquisition of more possessions, better jobs, a multitude of glamorous lovers, or greater and greater accomplishments, but rather in how we relate to the world.

Happiness can be found wherever we look, so long as we take a good look, and don't pass straight on to the Next Big Thing. The men in this book have looked long and hard, and found something which delights, inspires and perhaps even compels them.

In the 21st century, we tend to believe that the fast pace of life is a good thing, that boredom strikes when things remain the same. However, when we look closely at something, and allow ourselves to spend time experiencing it for what it is, the richness of each moment as it changes and flows into the next may take our breath away. We also tend to think that choice is a good thing, that having lots of options means we can select the one best suited to us. But the proliferation of choices offered to us, from cars to smartphones, from partners to what to watch on TV, actually paralyses us, leaving us miserable and filled with regret. The commoditisation of happiness is the greatest confidence trick ever played on our species, and the very things we are persuaded will make us happy actually make us miserable. Is it any surprise, then, that in a world richer and healthier than at any time in the past, we experience more and more depression?

So are the men featured in this book dull, or have they found serenity in a singular passion? Do we want to point a finger and laugh, or are we secretly jealous, knowing there is wisdom here, courage to break off from the herd, quietness and peace, and an engagement with beauty which only time and love can bring?

Because whether it is bricks, milk bottles, post boxes or roundabouts, the mundane contains much that is beautiful and fascinating, and I encourage everyone to read through the forty stories contained in this book and ask themselves, Where might I find happiness like that?

Dr Coulson
Middlesex University
2015

Welcome to our Dull Men's Club book. Far from glitz and glam, it's about enjoying everyday, mundane, humdrum things. We are not fast and furious. We're slow and steady. Our motto is 'Celebrating the Ordinary'.

We find that satisfaction comes in doing what needs to be done each day – routine, unglamorous activities, chores, errands.

We do not spend our weekends sky diving, wrestling alligators or running with the bulls. Instead, we repair vintage buses, grow giant vegetables or simply watch bread rise.

The DMC is not one of those typical aspirational programmes for men. We are not promising six-pack abs, faster running times, bald spots eliminated. We merely aspire to maintain our dullness – 'It's OK to Be Dull'.

Nor is the DMC one of those twelve-step programmes where members try to change. We are a two-step programme: (1) we admit we are dull; (2) we hope to keep it that way.

As you will notice, our book is free of exclamation marks (perhaps the only book ever like this). Exclamation marks are too exciting for us.

We hope you have as much fun reading this book as we have had writing it.

Sincerely (dull men are always sincere, mostly),

Leland Carlson
Assistant Vice President*
Dull Men's Club

* This is our highest office

A PRO AT WATCHING PAINT DRY KEITH JACKSON

It was a job that dull men everywhere would love to have: watching paint dry. Keith Jackson, now retired, used to work at a paint manufacture company, AquaTec Coatings, in Wrexham, North Wales. He was the company's technical manager, in charge of paint development and production.

Knowing how long paint takes to dry is very important. For example, AquaTec Coatings makes the paint for the London Underground train stations. Here, the trains stop running at 3 a.m. and start up again at 5 a.m. It was important that Keith watched the paint to make sure it was dry within the very short time window, so that passengers could walk on it in the morning without getting stuck.

Equipment needs for the job of watching paint dry are not excessive: all that's required is patience and a stopwatch. Keith even used to judge the drying by touching the paint with a finger. Drying time is not the most important aspect of paint development. Knowing how the paint will perform once it is dry is also very critical.

'I used to get wisecracks from people passing by and seeing what I was doing,' Keith says. 'One asked, "Can I give you a hand?" I replied, "No, not really, one of your fingers will be enough".'

In his spare time, Keith is surprisingly happiest scrambling up mountains, kayaking, diving, and touring around Europe with his wife in their caravan.

APOSTROPHE PROTECTOR JOHN RICHARDS

John Richards founded the Apostrophe Protection Society to combat the widespread incorrect use of the apostrophe – to preserve correct use of this much-abused punctuation mark.

The society's website shows examples of apostrophe misuse and abuse and suggests corrections. Richards has put together a standard letter that politely explains the basic rules for apostrophe usage. He sends the letter to supporters to forward to offending 'apostrophisers'.

John has been recognised for his work, winning an Ig Nobel Prize in Literature in 2001 for his 'efforts to protect, promote and defend the differences between plural and possessive'.

When we went to photograph him in a suitable setting he asked, 'What on earth do you want to take photo of – an apostrophe?'

We suggested we look for signs that were not using apostrophes correctly. 'There used to be some but we've got them corrected,' he said.

We went out for a walk anyway and, sure enough, found some new mistakes.

BAKELITE BUFF PATRICK COOK

Patrick Cook is an archaeologist of ordinary, everyday objects, mostly made from Bakelite, the world's first synthetic plastic to be mass-produced. Located in a watermill in Williton, a village in the peaceful Somerset countryside, The Bakelite Museum is home to Patrick's vast collection. The watermill has been designated by English Heritage as a Grade II listed building. The water wheel is still in place.

Among the fascinating items in the museum are radios, TVs, telephones, doll's house furniture, dental implants, caravans, and even a coffin. Many of them are Art Deco, the prevalent style in the heyday of Bakelite, and are brown (perhaps one of the reasons why dull men are drawn to the museum?).

Patrick has been acquiring these items since 1973. He finds them in street markets, boot fairs and junk shops. The collection now has 19,786 objects. With kind donations, it is continually expanding.

Summing up the museum, a visitor wrote on a travel website, 'making ordinary beautiful' – right up our alley, as our motto is 'Celebrating the Ordinary'.

Visiting the museum brings back many memories for those of us who grew up with Bakelite. Another memory brought back is the career advice Dustin Hoffman received in *The Graduate*: 'I just want to say one word to you – just one word – plastics.'

BAKER PROVING A POINT RICHARD COPSEY

The act of turning a hobby into a burgeoning business is a delight to see, especially if the business is something rather straightforward and ordinary. Former schoolteacher, Richard Copsey, along with his partner Kate, has done just that.

Richard and Kate love to bake. They began baking bread and cakes in their kitchen on weekends and selling them to a small group of friends. After doing this for a year, the demand outgrew the kitchen. They took the plunge – quit their day jobs and opened

their own shop, Holtwhites Bakery in Enfield, North London. It opened in July 2011 and dull men began dropping by almost immediately to watch the bread rise.

'A while back, when the Dull Men's Club came to film bread rising, I realised that in fact I like to watch bread rise too,' Richard explains. 'I rarely stand there continually while it is rising; instead I check on it from time to time as I'm attending to the many other things that need to be done in a bakery.

'I read about a famous chef in the US – Thomas Keller from The French Laundry in California – who said something that pertains to me. He feels comfortable doing the same thing over and over and over again, which is one of the reasons he became good at cooking. He didn't always have to be doing something new.

'Baking is a craft and a craft is doing the same thing each day, each day trying to do it better than the day before.'

BANDSTANDS OF BRITAIN PAUL RABBITTS

Paul Rabbitts, a qualified landscape architect, is passionate and obsessive about bandstands. In fact, he has come to be a leading expert on them.

After earning a master's degree in landscape architecture at Edinburgh University, he began working on various park projects, initially in Jersey and then Carlisle.

Paul then moved back to his native North East and became head of the Landscape and Countryside Development team at Middlesbrough Council. He became interested in bandstands when he was working there on the restoration of Albert Park – and this was when the passion really took hold.

His first book on bandstands appeared in 2011. No one had written such a book before. It was also the time he started counting the UK's bandstands, somewhat to the dismay of his long-suffering wife Julie. The counting he began in Middlesbrough has ended up as the key database of www.bookaband-stand.com, a website and initiative that Paul is heavily involved with. Its goal is: 'Bringing Bandstands Back to Life'.

On his travels, he's always on the lookout for more bandstands. 'I still get so excited on visiting a new bandstand I haven't seen before,' he says, 'especially if it's a Walter Macfarlane 279 or 249 model.'

Paul and Julie live in Leighton Buzzard, Bedfordshire. Paul's 'day job' is head of parks and streets in Watford, Hertfordshire. He is trying to bring the town's only bandstand, which at the moment is leading an obscure life outside the town hall, back to life.

BEER CAN OBSESSIVE NICK WEST

Aged 16 – two years before he could legally buy them – Nick West started collecting beer cans. His collection grew slowly as he had to rely on his parents to buy him new cans 'as and when they remembered'.

It was Deborah (Nick's poor unsuspecting wife) who provided the unwitting catalyst for the 40-year obsession that followed. She found him the perfect Christmas gift – a book about beer can collecting. With renewed enthusiasm, Nick decided to specialise solely in British beer cans.

'Collecting British beer cans is perfect. There are usually about 150 to 250 new issues every year – just enough to keep me interested, but not too many to diminish that special buzz I get whenever I find a new can.

'All my cans are displayed in a specific order – by brewery, brand and date of release. This means that whenever I find a new can I am continually moving the others around. Sometimes it can take me over an hour to add a single can.'

He spent the past two years researching a catalogue of every British beer can ever produced since they were first introduced in Wales in 1936. So far he has identified more than 9,000 different cans. 'With 7,522 cans currently in my collection, this leaves a further 1,500 cans that I still need. However, a lot of these are old and extremely rare – some only exist in photographs. Collecting them all would be incredibly expensive, if not impossible.'

If you have any old or interesting British beer cans, Nick would love to hear from you: nicquest_uk@hotmail.com.

BRICK COLLECTOR NEIL BRITTLEBANK

Neil Brittlebank, a retired mine-safety officer, collects bricks. It started in 1996 when he heard that Rothwell colliery, near Leeds, which closed in 1984, was being considered as a site for a new Country Park; Neil had worked at the colliery for 16 years.

He visited the site and saw bricks lying around that were to be crushed to make ballast for a new access road into the site. He

was given permission to take some of the bricks. Many came from brickworks that had disappeared over the years, which made them even more interesting.

He feels that bricks are part of our industrial heritage and they deserve to be preserved. His oldest brick, from a company at Drighlington, near Leeds, dates back to 1889.

The collection, which now consists of 300 bricks, continues to develop. But Neil is always on the lookout for more: demolition sites, abandoned building and hedgerows are frequent sources. As is his front door, where from time to time people drop off a few.

COUNTRY COUNTER JEREMY BURTON

Throughout his life, Jeremy Burton has wondered whether there might be a disease called 'constant counting disorder'. If there is, he believes he has it. He blames his parents. They bought him his first stamp album and he has never looked back.

Collecting stamps was followed by cigarette cards, then Brooke Bond tea cards, I-Spy guides, London Transport bus tickets and bus numbers. Next came collecting Southern Region train numbers, with the help of Ian Allan trainspotters' guides.

When he grew up, Jeremy started a career in information technology, a job that provided justification for his travels, which began 50 years ago.

The constant counting continued. To date: 2,407,332 miles flown, more than 1,313 flights (366 on British Airways), 119 airlines, 239 airports, 115 countries, five continents. The number of countries will increase to over 120 when Jeremy visits Colombia, Finland in 2015 and the Caribbean.

Once Jeremy had visited 100 countries, which occurred as he crossed over the border from Nicaragua to Honduras in 2012, he was inducted into the International Travelers' Century Club, a place where international globetrotters meet – and bore each other to death talking about their travels.

Another aspect of Jeremy's travels that might seem dull is the extensive recordkeeping required to consolidate flight and country information, but he actually enjoys it. When Jeremy looks at a map he maintains and spots a country he's not yet visited, it doesn't take long for the urge to get up and go to kick in again.

When not circling the globe, Jeremy and his wife Maggie reside in the village of Shurlock Row, Berkshire.

CUCKOOLAND THE PIEKARSKI BROTHERS

Even though the native habitat of the cuckoo clock is the Black Forest in Germany, the world's foremost museum for them is in England – at Tabley in Cheshire, to be specific, only a mile and a half off the M6.

Cuckooland has more than 700 cuckoo clocks on display, each one different from the others. The museum was founded in 1990 by the Piekarski brothers, Roman and Maz. The brothers are first and foremost horologists; each of them trained for this in Manchester, starting at the age of 15.

At the museum, Roman handles publicity and administration while Max is the technician who maintains and repairs the clocks. They also are experienced clock restorers and have a clock-restoring business.

Two exceptionally busy days at the museum are when daylight-saving time begins and

ends. Although not all of the 700 clocks are running continuously, at least 250 of them are, which means they need to be changed twice a year. We in the Dull Men's Club are envious of Roman and Maz – we enjoy altering our clocks, it's safe excitement for us.

The Piekarskis are continually on the lookout for notable and rare cuckoo clocks. Recently they became very excited when they came across, and acquired, an 1880s clock made by renowned clockmaker Theodor Ketterer, of Furtwangen in the Black Forest. Its walnut case featured an amazingly high standard of carving.

DRAINSPOTTER ARCHIE WORKMAN

Archie Workman is unable to curb his passion for drain covers. The former foundry worker now works three days a month as a parish council lengthsman (a person who keeps a length of road tidy), maintaining verges, road signs and drains on back roads in South Cumbria, near where he lives in Ulverston. On his travels, he continually finds hidden drains that have not seen the light for years.

'I love finding drain covers and enjoy working in such a beautiful environment,' he says. 'There's great history behind every drain cover. Many have the foundries' names cast in them, foundries in Blackburn, Clitheroe, Preston and Ulverston. I find it sad that these great names lie there unrecognised.'

Archie has photographed many of the drains, amassing an unusual collection, which one day he hopes may form an interesting book.

'It is also interesting to me, as I am an engineer, to observe the geometry of the interconnecting pipes. There's a whole world going on underneath us that we do not know about.'

In 2014, Archie produced a calendar of drain covers as a joke for the Clerk of Colton Parish Council. It became an overnight sensation. Hundreds of people bought them. Sales proceeds were used to buy tools for cleaning the drain covers, and wild seeds.

Archie now gives talks about his 'drainspotting' to a wide range of organisations across the UK. The title of his talks? 'My Life in the Gutter'.

FILOFAX BLOGGER STEVE MORTON

Steve Morton co-ordinates a large community of enthusiastic Filofax users and collectors. He 'works' as a regular blogger with the team behind Philofaxy, a website dedicated to Filofax organisers, which he joined in 2009. As a result of his sterling work, he's now referred to as 'Mr Philofaxy' by fellow collectors.

Philofaxy readers meet in various cities around the world; they also interact via Skype, Facebook and Twitter (ironic, but in today's world they use modern methods of communicating as an adjunct to their love of pencil and paper). Steve attends these meetings and also liaises with the staff at Filofax and several other small organiser companies in Europe and the USA.

Steve first used a Filofax in 1986. Like most people, he drifted into using electronic devices in the early 1990s. But a change in job in 2005 saw him return to using a Filofax: the new job forbade the use of electronic devices.

He uses a Filofax even more now that he is retired from his job as a radio engineer and has moved to France. 'I find it quite relaxing to get away from my computer, mobile phone, tablet and all the other

electronics I use and to sit for some time each day with just paper and pen and my journal to write down my thoughts of the day,' Steve says.

FOLLY FAN GWYN HEADLEY

'Living overseas, we visited the UK for holidays, and when I was five the family picnicked by Broadway Tower in the Cotswolds,' Gwyn Headley says. 'This immense building stood solitary in a field, no road or path leading to it. It made no sense.'

It began to make sense when his father explained it was a folly, built for the sheer pleasure of building it. 'An alternative dimension opened up to me, one where fun wasn't rationed like everything else in the 1950s,' he adds.

The passion that began at the age of five not only survived the trials and tribulations of upbringing and education – it thrived:

- Gwyn has published five books and 40 e-books about follies.

- He founded the Folly Fellowship – 25 years ago.

- He continues to find more follies that fascinate him, most recently 'a cracker' at Fischbach in Germany.

'The thrill of finding new ones never diminishes,' says Gwyn. 'I wish I could explain it.'

Thrills from finding new follies? That sounds like what we in the Dull Men's Club call 'safe excitement', a safe activity for dull men. Actually, it's not all that dull. Spotting follies in fields is perhaps more exciting than spotting tubs in fields, an activity that some other dull men engage in.

Gwyn and his wife Yvonne live in Crouch End, North London. It's a lovely home with a stunning view of the city to the south – but only if you can tear yourself away from looking at the many amazing pictures of follies hanging throughout the house.

GOLF BALL GATHERER MARTYN VALLANCE

Martyn Vallance began collecting logo golf balls in August 1997 after his uncle, a greenkeeper, gave him a bag of them. He became intrigued with the logos – logos of golf clubs, tournaments, sports teams, corporate logos.

In the early years, Martyn acquired most of his golf balls by hunting for them on the local golf course and at car boot sales. Then he became a greenkeeper himself, which gave him another source. More recently, he began bidding for balls on eBay. And tweeting, which is producing a nice flow of balls from fellow Twitterers.

Martyn finds people are shocked at the sheer size of his collection and they think he's mad when he tells them he has more than 70,000 logo golf balls tucked away in his garden shed and attic. Needless to say, this does not faze him in the least.

His favourites tend to be the rarer centenary golf club balls, those from golf tournaments and the kind featuring sports team logos.

'The thrill of finding a new logo golf ball for my collection is just as big now as when I began,' Martyn says. 'And you just can't beat the feeling of a "lucky dip" box of logo balls from a golf ball dealer.'

Ironically, although he played golf when he was younger, he no longer plays due to work and family commitments.

Martyn, his wife Claire and their four-year-old daughter Chloe live in Bude, Cornwall. Eventually, they hope to move into a house with a garage so they can turn the garage into a golf ball museum.

GRAFFILTHI ARTIST RICK MINNS

Artist Rick Minns paints oil on canvas as well as doing murals and charcoal sketches. He lives in the village of Wicklewood in Norfolk.

He's also known as 'Ruddy Muddy', the van Gogh of muddy white vans – turning the mud into works of art. He calls it 'graffilthi art'.

Rick first started on his own van. Then, he noticed other vans with words in the mud on them, words he didn't think his kids should see, so he began covering those words with his graffilthi (graffiti on filthy vans).

He first sketches using a fingernail, then uses a finger or tissue. 'Once in a while, a cotton bud; that's as extravagant as it gets,' Rick says. It takes five minutes to an hour to do each one. Some of them are quite intricate. The first drawings were mountains. Then came surfers, children walking, children fishing, a carp, a battleship, Jack Dee and more.

'It's just nice to see the smiles on peoples' faces when they watch me doing this.'

More and more people who see what Rick can do with mud are commissioning him to do oil paintings and other artwork.

HANDSAW CURATOR SIMON BARLEY

Retired medical doctor Simon Barley is now one of the world's foremost authorities and curators of handsaws. His collection forms three quarters of the 2,000 handsaws now in the Hawley Tool Collection Saw Shop, a replica of a bygone shop in Sheffield's industrial Kelham Island Museum.

His story began when he was converting his 19th-century stone barn into a house. 'I became fascinated with all the wonderful hand tools I could use, especially the saws,' he says. 'Machine saws always frightened me but handsaws were a delight to use. I was able to feel the timber as I worked with it. Sawing the length of a long beam by hand was pure pleasure.'

Simon signed up for a PhD on the early saw-making industry in Sheffield. The PhD, which was completed in nine years, led to a book – *British Saws & Saw Makers from c1660* – that took another six years to complete. The 734-page book became, overnight, *the* bible of handsaws.

Thanks to his PhD, a unique opportunity landed in Simon's lap in 1998 when Ken Hawley (1927–2014) invited him to catalogue the saws and saw-making tools and materials in The Hawley Collection, an archive of more than 70,000 hand tools.

Simon and his wife have left the converted stone barn for a village west of Sheffield in Hope Valley in the Peak District. They have three children who, among other things, are accomplished musicians – violin, cello, and double bass, but no musical saws.

LAWN DIARIST DAVID GRISENTHWAITE

Known in the media as the 'Lawn Diarist', David Grisenthwaite has kept a diary of each time he has mown his lawn since 1984. The diary's methodical recordings (we dull men admire methodical endeavours) turned out to be important research material for studies of global warming being carried out by the Royal Meteorological Society. Although the time spent mowing varies year by year, the diary clearly shows that the average annual lawn-mowing period has increased by 1½ months in 31 years of recorded mowings.

Sticking to the task for so many years is quite an accomplishment (we dull men like sticktoit-iveness too), especially as David has come down with macular degeneration (damage to the macula, which is in the centre of an eye's retina, causing vision loss). He now uses a video magnifier to record mowings, as well as for other reading and writing.

The date David began recording is rather interesting. Not only the year, 1984, but also the day, which was 1 April.

'I didn't think I was doing anything out of the ordinary,' David, who lives in Kirkcaldy, Scotland, said when told about the monumental significance of his work.

LAWNMOWER COLLECTOR STAN HARDWICK

Collecting lawnmowers comes naturally to someone like Stan. He's a retired greenskeeper. More than that, Stan loves lawnmowers. He has over 400 in his collection, enough to use a different one each day of the year. He has practically every type of lawnmower imaginable in his collection, some from as far back as the 19th century.

Stan's father didn't have it so good. He could not afford a lawnmower, so he cut the small lawn at their home using a pair of hedge-cutting shears and a piece of carpet to protect his knees. It took several hours to do it this way.

Stan's wife Margaret allows his favourites into their front room. 'It's more convenient for visitors to see them,' Stan says. The rest are in a huge, two-storey shed at the bottom of their back garden.

The couple do not have a computer, but, once a week, they walk to their local library and use a computer there to look for lawnmowers on eBay. 'I still get a thrill when I find another one for my collection,' Stan says.

I fought the LAWN and the lawn WON

The Hardwicks live in Filey, Yorkshire, in a lovely home at the end of a quiet cul-de-sac with a well-groomed lawn out in front. Next to the house is a large sports field, three football pitches and a cricket field, where Stan can test his lawnmowers.

MILITARY VEHICLE RESTORERS RICHARD & DICK FRYER

Dick and his son Richard Fryer, from Crewkerne in Somerset, began restoring a Jeep in 1997. Dick had been storing two Jeeps, in various states of disrepair, in his garage since 1971. Using parts from each of these Jeeps, they managed to put together a complete, fully operational Jeep.

They finished with the Jeep in 2004. A year later they started on a Scammell recovery lorry. 'During that gap year, I found that I was lost for something to do in my spare time,' Richard says.

The two of them belong to the Military Vehicle Trust (MVT) and participate in the group's activities. They drive the Jeep on road runs, to shows and places of interest, such as The Tank Museum in Bovington and France for the MVT's D-Day Remembrance events.

Discussions arising in their work that might be of interest to dull men include which is the proper shade of olive drab for Jeeps and the correct type of threads for nuts and bolts. As a matter of fact, when we visited Dick and Richard, we had a fascinating discussion about British versus American thread shapes and sizes for nuts and bolts.

Dick, a retired thatcher, and Richard, a crane engineer, do all of the work on the vehicles themselves: stripping down, sand-blasting, painting, welding, rebuilding engine and gearboxes, and wiring. They specialise in World War II vehicles and regard themselves as purists, inasmuch as they restore each vehicle to be as it was when it came out of the factory.

MILK BOTTLE MUSEUM STEVE WHEELER

For 35 years, Steve Wheeler, retired cattle exporter, has been collecting milk bottles. He finds them at farms, dairies, scrap yards and antique shops all over the world. He also finds them online, at collectors' conventions, and swaps them with fellow collectors.

'The moment I hear of a unique bottle that's not yet in my museum [as he's dubbed his collection], I'm off,' Steve explains. 'Each bottle I find is different. There's a fascinating history behind each one.'

His collection, which now consists of 20,000 bottles, is housed in a 100ft long workshop he built behind his home in Malvern, Worcestershire. Some of his bottles date back to the 1860s.

He picked up his first bottle while hiking in Snowdonia, a dirty bottle with an old red telephone painted on it. He researched and found it was from the 1940s from the Goodwin Dairy in Whitchurch, Shropshire, a dairy that, like many other dairies, is no longer in existence.

'Ironically, I don't even like milk,' Steve says. 'But I do love glass. It's not just the bottles I love; it's also the thrill of finding them. And the people I meet when I'm collecting them.'

Steve's wife Sue accompanies him on bottle hunts. She's a retired accountant who dislikes clutter and loves cleanliness almost as much as Steve loves collecting. She teams up with Steve for the annual spring clean of the bottles.

If you find or want to get rid of old milk bottles, contact Steve: milkbottlespast@hotmail.com. He'll be happy to hear from you.

MODEL FOR ANORAKS STEVE RESZETNIAK

On retiring from the Inland Revenue, Steve Reszetniak was looking for a new career that would fit nicely into his lifestyle, persona and budget.

In what proved to be a light-bulb moment, he hit on the perfect idea – anorak model – while showering (where the best ideas are born) one morning: 'Most models are too glamorous to project the proper look when modelling anoraks,' Steve says. 'I fit the bill perfectly.'

Steve is currently interviewing for modelling work with manufacturers of anoraks as well as stores that sell them, particularly chains such as M&S, Debenhams and John Lewis. Not to mention catalogues. 'In

one of the interviews I was told, "You're the anorak of anoraks",' he says proudly.

Then there are the potential acting roles – trainspotter, drainspotter, cloud watcher, simply sitting on a bench. A TV series maybe? *Man Wearing Anorak*? *Trainspotter in Anorak*?

Most of the anoraks in Steve's collection are grey. There are a few beige ones and two in navy blue. And there's the red one that he wears on Valentine's Day and on his wife Anne's birthday.

'I just love it when Steve wears the red one, it gets me so excited,' says Anne. 'There will be even more excitement on my next birthday: we'll be getting matching anoraks.'

Steve and Anne live in Enfield, a lovely, quiet suburb at the north end of London. Anoraks are often spotted in the area.

MOUNTAIN MEASURERS JOHN BARNARD, GRAHAM JACKSON & MYRDDYN PHILLIPS

John Barnard, Graham Jackson and Myrddyn Phillips: three creative hill baggers who have heightened their walking experience with a fascinating goal – determining whether hills they are walking on are, in fact hills. Might they be mountains? To be classified as a mountain, a hill in Wales and England has to be 2,000ft or more above sea level (ODN/Ordnance Datum Newlyn).

The men target summits close to the 2,000ft mark, some over and some under. As Graham says, 'It's much more fun to upgrade a hill to a mountain than the other way around.' Any changes they think should be made – about three or four each year – are brought to the attention of the Ordnance Survey, who then come out to confirm the findings.

To accomplish this, the three hill walkers spent £10,000 on professional surveyor-grade GPS equipment, equipment that measures height accuracy to within 5cm. This is considerably more accurate than measurements appearing on modern maps made using aerial photography by Ordnance Survey. A representative from the survey said, 'We are quite happy with the work they are doing.'

When we at the club heard about this, we thought how much simpler – and safer – than mountain climbing. No ropes, carabiners or pickaxes to bother with; no need even to wear a helmet. Just measuring equipment with dials to play with.

'It brings together wonderful things like science and technology, health and fitness – in beautiful settings,' says Myrddyn.

PARK BENCH APPRECIATION SOCIETY
GROVER CLICK

Grover Click doesn't mind travelling – even if it's to exciting places – as long as he can find park benches when he gets there.

He enjoys sitting on a park bench and watching the rest of the world go by. It's a great way to get some fresh air – and benches are free.

Grover became enamoured of park benches while living in New York. He spent a great deal of time in Central Park. With its 8,500 benches, it's the park bench capital of the world.

'Benches come in many styles, often featuring the creative use of metals and wood,' Grover says. 'Some are pleasing to the eye, some complement the surrounding area, while others are simply there because a bench is needed at the location.

'Some are memorials. There's one for "The Park Bench Statesman" financier Bernard Baruch, long-time friend of Winston Churchill and Presidential Advisor to Franklin Roosevelt, in Lafayette Park in front of the White House. Advising on financial and government matters on park benches in Lafayette Park, as well as Central Park and St James's Park (see photo above), became his most famous characteristic.'

There's a memorial bench in Central Park for the late Cleveland Amory (*The Cat Who Came for Christmas* and *The Cat and the Curmudgeon*). He belonged to the New York Athletic Club – where Grover and I formed the Dull Men's Club – and was amused by and a mentor for what we were starting.

If you'd like to share photos of your favourite park benches, please post them on the Park Bench Appreciation Society Facebook group or email them to parkbenches@dullmensclub.com.

PLAQUE APPRECIATION SOCIETY MICK CHESTER

Mick Chester lives in East Cowes, a small town on the Isle of Wight. Following early retirement due to ill health and severe mobility problems, he took up photography. He started putting his photos on social media sites and joining other hobby photographer groups.

'Then I joined the Dull Men's Club on Facebook and found their Park Bench Appreciation Society page,' Mick says. 'I would head out on my mobility scooter photographing park benches.

'I also noticed historic plaques. I started photographing them. As I couldn't find a place to submit these photos, I formed The Plaque Appreciation Society, and it too has a page on Facebook.'

Mick became hooked on plaques, their many different shapes, sizes and styles. 'Some are made of stone, others from brass or cast iron,' he says. 'Each has its own story to tell.'

Plaques, he explains, can be found on houses commemorating a famous person who once lived there. Others on a building describing an event that took place there. Rather exciting are those set on plinths that mark the spot where something happened – for example, that in 1899 a man in East Cowes was fined for speeding – driving his motor wagonette at over 8 mph.

Mick had not realised just how many plaques are out there. Despite having photographed a lot of plaques on the island so far, he believes he will be doing this for a long time yet: 'My journey has just begun.'

POST BOX PHOTOGRAPHER PETER WILLIS

Retired Worcester postman and member number 2744 of the Letter Box Study Group, Peter Willis combines his interest in photography and travel by touring around the UK photographing the iconic boxes. He has photographed more than 2,500 of them over the past 10 years, his pictures revealing their history and surroundings.

'It's a great way to see our country and meet interesting local people who sometimes wonder what on earth I am up to,' Peter explains. 'They often provide new information such as boxes that are not in use anymore. Varying conditions, be they poor weather or vehicles and people "in the way", make the photography challenging at times, which adds to the enjoyment.'

Peter's son Steve has programmed the locations of the 115,000 post boxes in the UK into a handheld GPS unit that beeps each time it gets near one.

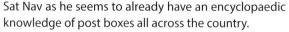

When talking with Peter, one wonders why he needs the Sat Nav as he seems to already have an encyclopaedic knowledge of post boxes all across the country.

Peter still gets 'a little thrill' each time he photographs a post box. He says, 'I've learnt it won't be possible to "bag them all", but I'm always looking for the next one. I get a kick from crossing them off my list.'

Peter is supported by his wife Dianne, who is very patient with his hobby and the amount of time it takes up.

POSTAL MUSEUM IN A SHED CURATOR
STEVE KNIGHT

Fifty-year-old marketing director Steve Knight, member number 1788 of the Letter Box Study Group, began collecting authentic cast-iron mail boxes 20 years ago. 'I saw one in an antique shop and thought it would look nice in my garden,' Steve says. 'I now have 127 of them.'

When the number of post boxes reached 15, he set up the Colne Valley Postal History Museum in his garden and shed.

Interestingly, the shed was voted Best Summerhouse Shed in the 2012 Shed of the Year competition hosted by website Readers Sheds.

The museum now spreads over two large sheds and most of Steve's suburban garden in the small Essex market town of Halstead.

'It houses my own special museum of all things postal,' Steve says proudly. 'It has post boxes and stamp-vending machines, of course, as well as cap badges, uniforms, telegram forms, water jugs, fire extinguishers, collection plates, direction signs, point-of-sale displays, string, scissors, knives, pencils, dip pens, ink wells, stained glass and scales. In fact just about anything with the magic letters GPO emblazoned on it can find its way into the museum.'

The shed is fully wired for power and telephone/internet. It could, theoretically, act in every way and function as a real post office. 'If our town post office closes, perhaps I'll open up here,' quips Steve.

QUEUE GURU TERRY GREEN

Queuing – it's right up there with watching paint dry on the list of things we like to do for safe excitement.

Terry Green, 'Mr Queue', has done much, probably more than anyone else, to make our queuing experiences even more enjoyable. For it was he who introduced the much-needed and improved order and fairness to our queuing experience.

You've probably heard Terry numerous times, although you were never aware of it. 'Cashier number three, please' – that's him. He's the voice heard 30,000 times every month at queues in Royal Mail post offices, banks, supermarkets and many other businesses and stores throughout the UK.

Terry is a queue management expert – a queue guru, if you like. Having studied queuing behaviour for many years, he has a virtual scrapbook of anecdotes about bad queuing experiences. 'Everyone I meet seems to have a queuing story,' he says.

I queue, therefore I am

Terry Green

He helped form a company that developed his system in the 1990s, a system now used by 55,000 businesses in 120 countries – that's a faster and fairer customer service for roughly a quarter of the world's population.

Those of us who always seem to pick the wrong queue when at a store that uses traditional multiple queues are most grateful when we find ourselves in one of Terry's queues.

RAIL TIMETABLE COMPILER JOHN POTTER

John Potter is the rescuer of the European Rail Timetable. Published for 140 years by Thomas Cook, the timetable ceased in August 2013 due to the company's downsizing and cost-cutting measures.

Trainspotters were devastated.

Also disappointed were the many rail travellers who relied upon the timetables for route planning and the armchair travellers who depended on them for entertainment.

The *Thomas Cook European Rail Timetable*, the 'rail bible', supplied travellers with schedules for 50,000 train, bus and ferry connections in 5,000 locations throughout Europe.

John has been part of the timetable editorial team since 1998. He wanted to continue working on it – so he bought the rights to the timetable as well as the timetable-compiling software from the company, using part of his redundancy payment and re-mortgaging his house to finance his new start-up.

Publishing of the revived timetable, now entitled the *European Rail Timetable*, began in March 2014. Its publications can be ordered on europeanrailtimetable.eu.

'I am not a wordsmith, I just like numbers,' says John. 'When working on the timetable I have to manually enter the train numbers and times for each station on all the routes. Some people think numbers are dull, I find them interesting.'

Avid timetable users say that a timetable on an iPhone or an Android doesn't provide the same browsability as a 600-page printed timetable – there's not the same alluring presentation of routes, times, maps and scenic routes. By flicking through a paper timetable, readers devise journeys and enjoy the serendipity of discovering train services they never knew existed.

ROMANTIC HERO KEN McCOY

The Valentine's Day card Ken McCoy gave to his wife Valerie in 1978, the fourth year of their marriage, has been reused every year after that.

'I'm still thrilled to bits each time I receive it. I am always looking forward to seeing what Ken writes in it next,' Val says.

Ken designed the card himself. Before becoming a writer of crime and romance novels, he was a card designer, designing hundreds of cards for Hallmark and other big companies.

As for the new messages Ken writes in the card every year… 'There's room for many more,' he says. 'Enough until we are at least 150.'

He always puts the card back in a safe place. One year the place was so safe it took Ken quite a while to find it again, but find it he did.

Ken is a popular after-dinner speaker. He lives with Valerie in Leeds. He regards himself as a romantic, not a penny-pincher.

ROUNDABOUT APPRECIATION SOCIETY
KEVIN BERESFORD

Often called 'Lord of the Rings', Kevin Beresford is president of the UK Roundabout Appreciation Society (UKRAS), a society he founded in 2003.

'UKRAS members see a roundabout as an oasis on a sea of asphalt,' Kevin explains. 'Roundabouts, with their infinite variety of designs, colours and inventiveness, lift sagging spirits on long, tiresome journeys.'

Kevin is regarded by TV and radio presenters and newspaper reporters as an authority on roundabouts and related traffic matters. He has published two books – *Roundabouts of Great Britain* and *Roundabouts from the Air*. He travels throughout Great Britain year-round to find more fascinating roundabouts to photograph for his annual calendar, *Best of British Roundabouts*.

'Local councils are proud of their roundabouts,' Kevin is keen to point out. 'They plant beautifully landscaped gardens in the middle of them. Or put practically anything else on them. I've seen roundabouts with trains, boats, planes, pubs, churches, pump-houses, working windmills, duck ponds, knights in armour, giant barometers, giant cockerels, giant mosquitoes, shepherds and their flocks, fountains, topiaries, statues, laser and light shows…'

UKRAS meets every other month at The Bramley Cottage, a pub in Redditch.

SEA WALL PROTECTOR MICHAEL KENNEDY

Michael Kennedy, who lives in Hunstanton on the Norfolk coast, spends two hours every day, except Saturdays, moving rocks to build a sea wall along the coast. The sea wall protects the cliffs along Hunstanton's coast from eroding.

He's been doing this for over 20 years and does it all by himself.

'I used to walk to Old Hunstanton and back, 21 miles every day, but that wasn't enough physical exercise for me,' Michael says. 'I started moving rocks and now I can't stop. It's better than sitting in the armchair and I'll do it for as long as I'm healthy.'

What about Saturdays? He takes a day off to watch sports on TV. He's a Chelsea fan.

Michael is adored by local residents. 'He's the sort of character who makes the British seaside what it is,' Hunstanton Mayor Peter Mallam said in 2011.

We agree. He's doing something that's routine and unglamorous – doing it methodically and continually day after day. He's not doing it for glory either: he's out there alone, with no one cheering him on.

And he's accomplishing something important to boot – saving the coastline.

SUBURBAN RAMBLER MARTYN SHOULER

Martyn Shouler noticed at an early age that he was prone to rather mild obsessions – he had become interested in stationery, maps, cameras, the Underground and London's suburbs.

A little later, when studying in London for a master's degree in communication design, he began taking photos of Underground stations. He also enjoyed meeting people with spectacularly mundane interests – collecting shopping lists, following flight paths on a pushbike, drawing portable gas heaters. It was indeed an inspiring time for Martyn.

He continued the ordinary lifestyle with a series of long and pointless walks in and around London. Initially these were for no other reason than to work up a good thirst, but eventually he decided to plot them on a wall map for his own amusement. He carried a camera and began to document something in each postal district within the M25.

Eventually he began assembling photos of shop frontages, something he's particularly excited about. 'I process them in black and white to maintain an overall subdued mood, which I feel is befitting,' he says. There are now 70 photos in the collection.

His newest project is Project Dismal. 'It's still in its infancy, but at least it's a good excuse to justify a nice new anorak,' he says. It came about when he found himself taking photos of dismal early-morning scenes when photographing shop frontages.

Martyn now lives in Bedford. He is no longer married. 'My ex-wife thought I was incredibly boring. It was the one thing we could agree on,' he says.

TAX DISC FANATIC JUDE CURRIE

A 13-year-old car enthusiast who began collecting tax discs in 2009 now has close to 15,000 in his collection.

Jude Currie began the collection after spotting an abandoned Fiat in 2009. Something caught his eye – the tax disc on the windscreen. The next day he went with his father to a scrapyard and got 30 more. The rest, as they say, is history.

Jude says his favourites are from the 60s, 70s and 80s. 'They have interesting colours and are very well designed,' says Jude. His earliest one is from 1926. 'I see tax discs as part of the history of motoring in Britain and it is a pity they have now been phased out.'

Jude's father, Garnet, who says he's never been a car person, is continually impressed with his son's fabulous knowledge of the car industry. 'If he went on *Mastermind*, his category would be British Leyland or cars from the Eastern bloc,' Garnet says of his son.

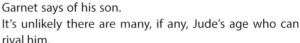

It's unlikely there are many, if any, Jude's age who can rival him.

Although not old enough to drive legally, Jude already owns a car. In 2012, Garnet and Jude went to a classic car show, where Jude entered a £1 draw for a Trabant car. He won it. 'It's a great car,' he says.

TOY SOLDIERS TIM BARKER

Tim Barker is an actor. He actually played the character 'The Dull Man' in the film *Calendar Girls* (2003). He's also been in many other films and in most of the British soaps.

He has collected toy soldiers for 50 years. It first began when his father gave him *Little Wars* by H.G. Wells, a book of rules for playing with toy soldiers.

Tim now lives back in his hometown of Silloth, a seaside holiday resort in Cumbria. He set up a museum for his toy soldiers, 'Soldiers in Silloth', and a website: www.soldiersinsilloth.co.uk.

Many of the toys in his collection have been acquired from all over the world while Tim has been away for work, including places as far afield as Australia, China, Egypt, Lebanon, and the former Soviet Union and Yugoslavia, and some are over a century old. In addition to soldiers, there are toy vehicles, catapults, chariots, tanks, canons, guns, forts and castles. Periods depicted in the collection include Ancient Egypt, Hadrian's Wall (Silloth is near the wall), Waterloo and the Napoleonic Wars, the American Civil War, and the World Wars. Tim also has Victorian lead soldiers, like the ones Winston Churchill played with as a boy, in his collection. But he also has modern plastic toy soldiers like the ones in *Toy Story*, to add to his growing number.

TRAFFIC CONE COLLECTOR DAVID MORGAN

'Nothing warms David's heart more than a traffic cone,' the *Oxford Mail* reported of David Morgan, from Burford, Oxfordshire, who is listed in *Guinness World Records* as having the world's largest traffic cone collection.

David is sales director of a plastics company that manufactures traffic cones. His collection began in 1986 as a result of a legal dispute with a rival manufacturer over the design of a cone. He searched all over the UK for cones that proved his company's had not been copied from a cone designed by the rival. David won the case and that was just the start.

'Once I started collecting cones, I wasn't able to stop,' he says. 'I find out where roadworks are and go and look for cones. Everywhere I go, I collect them. It's really interesting. There are so many different shapes, sizes and colours. And the models are always changing. The best ones come from village halls and undertakers. Undertakers look after their cones.'

The oldest cone in the collection – David's prize possession – is a 1956 Lynvale rubber cone from Scotland.

Two other notables are the one from Malaysia he found washed up on a beach in Sicily and a rare 1980 Adapterform model, which he picked up at the airport while on his honeymoon on the island of Corsica in 1988.

Andrew Dowd has visited all 2,548 railway stations in England, Scotland and Wales. It took him four years to complete this epic journey, beginning in early 2009 and finishing at the end of 2013.

To achieve what wouldn't be everyone's idea of fun he drove a total of 36,000 miles, visiting stations in regional batches, sometimes as many as 100 stations a day. Had he not grouped them but instead driven to each station and back, he estimates he would have driven 600,000 miles.

The idea came to mind when Andrew was looking at a family photograph and spotted a railway station sign in the background. He became curious and started photographing more station signs. At first he set out to do this for stations in the Greater Manchester area only, which is where he lives and teaches maths. Completing this task didn't take very long, so he extended his search and just kept going.

Ironically, Andrew did this by car. He found that travelling by car was less expensive and faster.

His routine was always the same: plan a route, pack a camera, hop into his car.

Normally, Andrew wouldn't spend much time at each station. 'Most of them are not all that interesting,' he says. 'Some, however, are, like St Pancras. I spent several hours there. I also took time in the far north of Scotland to take in the beautiful scenery.'

TRIG BAGGER ROB WOODALL

The world's leading trig bagger, no one has 'bagged', or visited, more trigs than Rob Woodall. His goal is to visit all 6,100 surviving trig pillars in Britain.

He has about 20 more to go, about 1,000 ahead of his nearest rival.

Trigs – triangulation points – which make up the Ordnance Survey's national grid of reference points on the tops of hills, are usually marked by waist-high pillars. Before aerial surveying, they were used by mapmakers and surveyors. Between 1936 and 1962, the Ordnance Survey placed 6,500 trig pillars right across the UK.

Before trig bagging, Rob was a hill bagger. He started bagging hills in 1980, but in 2001 it dawned on him that that trigs too were a 'tickable commodity'.

'Exploring the countryside is something I'm really fond of,' he explains. 'There's a trig point standing about every five kilometres as you move across Britain. Tracking them has allowed me to arrive in places I would otherwise never have been. I'm also motivated by being the first person to visit each of the trig points.'

Rob maintains a list of trig baggers who have reached their 1,000th trig mark. The list indicates the 1,000th pillar they reached.

'It's all good fun,' he says.

Rob lives in Peterborough, Cambridgeshire. He works as a waste-water modeller in his day job, finding solutions to eliminate problems arising from sewage flooding and pollution.

VACUUM CLEANER COLLECTOR JAMES BROWN

When someone says their job sucks, they don't usually mean it literally. But James Brown does. His work, as well as his hobby, revolves around vacuum cleaners – all aspects of these dust-collecting apparatus – selling new and reconditioned ones, repairing broken ones, collecting a wide variety of them.

James was a child prodigy in vacuuming. He started the activity aged four, and had his own vacuum cleaner by the age of eight.

He now holds the Guinness World Record for the largest collection, having more than 300 vacuum cleaners in his collection. Surprisingly, he is the first person to set a Guinness World Record for the world's largest collection of vacuum cleaners.

James took a holiday to the States a few years ago. Most Brits, when they go to America, visit places like Florida, California, the Grand Canyon and New York City. James visited Cleveland. Why? Because that's where his favourite vacuum cleaner, the Kirby, is made.

Dull men love to vacuum. It's such a practical thing to do. We love doing what needs to be done. Moreover, in one sense it beats watching paint dry – opportunities to vacuum arise more often.

When we visited James's shop recently, his new 100th-anniversary model of the Kirby had just arrived. He was over the moon.

VEGETABLE GIANTS PETER GLAZEBROOK

Peter Glazebrook thinks big when it comes to vegetables. He has been growing giant prize-winning vegetables in his garden at Halam in Nottinghamshire for 25 years.

The goal at first was vegetables judged on features such as shape and colour. Peter began to notice his vegetables were bigger and heavier than those from other contestants. So he started entering giant vegetable competitions.

Peter has held 15 Guinness World Records over the years. He currently holds three: cauliflower, potato and carrot.

In September 2014, one of his carrots, a 20-pounder, broke the world record for the heaviest carrot ever to be grown. The previous world record was set in 1988.

In April 2014, a 60lb, 6ft in diameter cauliflower he grew also broke the world record, the previous world record having been set in 1999. The average cauliflower weighs between one and three pounds. A 60lb cauliflower, after some serious chopping, breaks down into 120 portions.

Peter continually receives an immense amount of press, TV and radio coverage. The secret of his success? Heat, light and soil are key ingredients in the production of giants. A long growing season is also needed.

Seeds are important, too. Peter has developed his own seeds, some of which he shares with fellow growers. Ironically, this sometimes results in him being beaten by his own seeds.

Probably the most important thing for vegetable magnitude, however, is TLC, constant attention and nurturing. It's a full-time job. Peter and his wife Mary work 24/7. Holidays or even days away are out of the question.

VINTAGE BUS ENTHUSIAST STEVE MORRIS

Steve Morris has long been a bus enthusiast. He remembers lying in bed with measles when he was five and hearing buses passing by. He began to realise each bus made its own unique noise, had its own voice, its own personality – some wore smiley faces, some were grumpy, others quiet in their manner.

Steve is a trained hydraulics engineer. He had his own company that made hydraulic excavators for railway lines, which he sold in 2004. More importantly, he's recognised as an authority on buses.

He began collecting buses in 1974. At one point he had 30 of them. He's scaled back a bit. He now has 18, 14 of which are operable, four are being restored. Five of the operable ones are commercially registered – used by Steve's company, Quantock Heritage, for private hire for events like weddings and corporate events, and even funerals – the body rides in its casket on a bus.

'When working on a bus, I don't want to finish,' Steve says. 'I just want to keep on working. The fun is in the doing. It's like putting a jigsaw puzzle together: once the last piece is put in its place, the fun is over.'

Steve's buses are housed in buildings in Wiveliscombe, Somerset, where he lives. The shop where he maintains and restores his buses is next to his house – so close he can practically fall out of bed into his garage.

WORLD WAR I BUFF TONY COOKE

Tony Cooke came to our attention when we heard he had a tank on the front drive of his home in Cottenham, Cambridgeshire.

The tank is a Mark IV British Army tank, a replica of tanks used in the Great War. It's 13ft wide, 21ft long and weighs 6½ tonnes.

The glamour of driving a tank around town is only a small aspect of having a tank. Tony and his mate Kevin Jepson put in countless hours of painstaking, tedious work to restore the tank. 'This might sound dull, but not as dull as visitors who count the rivets to make sure they are even on each side,' Tony's wife, Gill, says.

Another aspect of Tony's passion is scouring battlefields, mostly in France, looking for artefacts. 'It can take hours to find only a few shell fragments, perhaps also things like a top to a beer bottle,' he explains.

Tony, Kevin and a few cohorts have built the National Centre for the Great War in Cambridge, a living history museum, privately financed and operated, which opens in 2015. The museum's goal is to educate people about, and keep alive, the history of World War I.

In addition to the tank, which will take centre stage, the centre will have examples outdoors of trenches, tunnels and narrow gauge railway which were part of the war. It will also have indoor facilities for learning, a shop and a café.

'It'll be a relief to my neighbours when the tank leaves my front drive,' Tony smiles.

WELL-KNOWN MEN WITH DULL TENDENCIES

Socrates, for example. He led a frugal, spartan life. He walked around Athens in a simple robe and no shoes. Nothing exciting about that, right? Moreover, he often went to the market place – the bazaar – to look at the many magnificent items for sale. He said, 'I love to go there to discover how many things I am perfectly happy without.'

Thomas Jefferson provides another example. He loved vanilla ice cream (our favourite flavour). He first tasted it in France; he brought home the recipe. The recipe is now in the US Library of Congress.

Sir Edmund Hillary considered himself just an ordinary beekeeper and, despite his great achievements, he lived life with exemplary humility.

Keith Richards has always been a bookworm. Early in life, his ambition was to be a librarian. He has achieved his goal now as he has large libraries at his homes in England and in Connecticut, USA.

Rod Stewart is an avid model-railway enthusiast. He has been on the covers of model railway magazines numerous times.

When England footballer Alan Shearer was asked, after his team Blackburn Rovers won the Premier League title from Manchester United, what he would be doing to celebrate, he said: 'I'm going home to creosote the fence.'

Mike Tyson has kept and bred pigeons from an early age. When he was 10 he won his first fight, a fight with a bully who killed one of his pigeons right in front of him. 'They teach you a lot about yourself,' Tyson says of his birds.

Celebrate the Ordinary

DMC

DULL MEN'S CLUB

50 Shades of Grey

50 SHADES OF GREY

1	2	3	4	5
6	7	8	9	10
11	12	13	14	15
16	17	18	19	20
21	22	23	24	25
26	27	28	29	30
31	32	33	34	35
36	37	38	39	40
41	42	43	44	45
46	47	48	49	50

FREQUENTLY ASKED QUESTIONS

1. Is the DMC a movement?
   No. We stay put.

2. Is the DMC fighting for some sort of 'rights'?
   No. We've never had anyone interfere with our right to remain dull.

3. What's the greatest accomplishment of the DMC and its members?
   Remaining dull in spite of the many distractions we face today – temptations to do exciting things.

4. Are dull men the same as boring men?
   Yes and no. Boring men are dull men. But not all dull men are boring men. Boring men are dull men who don't know when to stop; they go on and on.

5. Besides boring men, are there other types of dull men?
   Yes. A type that's at the other end of the spectrum are what we refer to as extroverted dull men. An example is one we know of who, when he's talking with you, is not looking down at his shoes. He's looking at *your* shoes.

6. Are dull men the same as nerds?
   No. Nerds do nerdy things like wear a glasses strap or a plastic shirt pocket protector for pens and pencils.

7. Are dull men the same as grumpy old men?
   No. Grumpy old men continually complain. Dull men don't complain in the same way as grumpy old men. Dull men do complain about certain things, however, like a TV or radio being too loud.

8. Are dull men idle?

   No. Dull men are not idle. Dull men do things – ordinary, everyday things that need to be done. They particularly like to do routine things. They enjoy making to-do lists and the thrill of ticking things off the list when they are done.

9. What's a good gift to give a dull man?

   Slippers.

10. Do dull men have a favourite colour?

    Yes. Grey. Beige is runner-up.

11. Do dull men have a favourite flavour?

    Yes. Vanilla.

12. What's a favourite book for a typical dull man?

    A dictionary. Words are nicely arranged in order in dictionaries.

13. What's the one thing dull men do best?

    Nap.

14. What's a favourite type of vacation for a dull man?

    Staycation.

15. Test: How can a man know whether he qualifies to become a member of the DMC?

    If he's read as far as this page, it's likely he qualifies.

ARE YOU A DULL MAN?

1. Have you ever had an urge? Were you able to get over it?

2. Is grey one of your favourite colours?

3. What are the three most exciting things you have ever done? It's OK if you list fewer than three. Did you list three or fewer things?

4. What are the three dullest things you have done? You can list more than three? Did you list three or more things?

5. When you say hello to someone you've met before, have they ever replied, 'I don't remember meeting you' and you reply, 'That's OK, I wouldn't remember meeting me either.'

6. List the dull places you have visited. Did you list one or more?

7. Do you like to watch airport luggage carousels?

8. List the dull books you have read. Did you list more than one book?

9. Is macaroni and cheese your favourite pasta dish?

10. Do you like Marmite and/or Vegemite?

11. Do you like airplane food (economy class)?

12. Is rice pudding one of your favourite desserts?

13. Does your wife or girlfriend think you are dull?

14. Do you know two dull men who are willing to sponsor you?

DMC MEMBERSHIP – HOW TO APPLY

Dull Men's Club

Men who feel they qualify and would like to be a member of the DMC can email us at:

membership4dullmen@dullmensclub.com

Or, if you would like to nominate someone you think qualifies, you can email the nomination to us using the same email address.

A membership certificate will be emailed to you.

Friends of Dull Men

If you are a friend of dull men and would like a 'Friend of Dull Men Certificate', please email us at:

membership4friendsofdullmen@dulmensclub.com.

A certificate will be emailed to you.

Website and contact us

Website: dullmensclub.com

Email: contactus@dullmensclub.com

Certificate of Membership

THE DULL MEN'S CLUB IS PLEASED TO LET IT BE KNOWN THAT

Tom Bland

IS A MEMBER IN GOOD STANDING OF THE DULL MEN'S CLUB, HAS DEMONSTRATED
NOTICEABLE SKILLS AT CELEBRATING THE ORDINARY, AND IS HEREBY CERTIFIED DULL

Leland Carlson
ASSISTANT VICE PRESIDENT*

Grover Click
ASSISTANT VICE PRESIDENT*

*ASSISTANT VICE PRESIDENT IS THE HIGHEST OFFICE OF THE DULL MEN'S CLUB

Photography

With special thanks to: AquaTec Coatings Ltd, Bayless Media Ltd, Emily Bentgen, Peter Bøjrstad, Maggie Burton, Leland Carlson, Tony and Gill Cooke, Benjamin Dee-Shapland, Lucy Feltham, Garnet Currie Photography, Getty Images, Mary Glazebrook, Gwyn and Yvonne Headley, McQueen's Male Grooming, Rick Minns, Tom Myers, James J. O'Brien, Ellie Rabbitts, Steve and Anne Reszetiak, Robert Merhaut Photography, Pinnacle Photo Agency Ltd, Jonathan Sears-Corfield, Martyn Shouler, Studio Stratford, Emma West, Nick West, Peter Willis and Yorkshire Post.

Agent, editor and designer

Also special thanks to Literary Agent Tim Bates (Pollinger/PFD), Commissioning Editor Sara Cywinski (Ebury Press/Penguin Random House) and Designer Ed Pickford (e-type).

The men

And a huge thanks to the men in this book, who are clearly showing the world that 'It's OK to Be Dull'.